**READERS**

READING
3
ALONE

Boys' Life SERIES

Nature
Detectives

Written by K. C. Kelley

DK Publishing

A Note

DK READERS is a compelling program for beginning readers, designed in conjunction with leading literacy experts, including Dr. Linda Gambrell, Distinguished Professor of Education at Clemson University. Dr. Gambrell has served as President of the National Reading Conference and the College Reading Association, and is President of the International Reading Association.

Beautiful illustrations and superb full-color photographs combine with engaging, easy-to-read stories to offer a fresh approach to each subject in the series. Each DK READER is guaranteed to capture a child's interest while developing his or her reading skills, general knowledge, and love of reading.

The five levels of DK READERS are aimed at different reading abilities, enabling you to choose the books that are exactly right for your child:

Pre-level 1: Learning to read
Level 1: Beginning to read
Level 2: Beginning to read alone
Level 3: Reading alone
Level 4: Proficient readers

The "normal" age at which a child begins to read can be anywhere from three to eight years old. Adult participation through the lower levels is very helpful for providing encouragement, discussing storylines, and sounding out unfamiliar words.

No matter which level you select, you can be sure that you are helping your child learn to read, then read to learn!

LONDON, NEW YORK, MUNICH,
MELBOURNE, AND DELHI

Publisher Beth Sutinis
Editor Brian Saliba
Custom Publishing Director Mike Vacarro
Managing Art Director Michelle Baxter

Reading Consultant
Linda Gambrell, Ph.D.

Produced by
Shoreline Publishing Group LLC
President James Buckley, Jr.
Designer Tom Carling, carlingdesign.com

The Boy Scouts of America®, Cub Scouts®,
Boys' Life®, and rank insignia are registered
trademarks of the Boy Scouts of America.
Printed under license from the
Boy Scouts of America.

First American Edition, 2007
07 08 09 10 11 10 9 8 7 6 5 4 3 2 1
Published in the United States by DK Publishing
375 Hudson Street, New York, New York 10014

Copyright © 2007 Dorling Kindersley Limited

Published in Great Britain by Dorling Kindersley Limited

DK books are available at special discounts when purchased in bulk
for sales promotions, premiums, fund-raising, or educational use.
For details, contact:
DK Publishing Special Markets,
375 Hudson Street, New York, New York 10014
SpecialSales@dk.com

A catalog record for this book is available
from the Library of Congress.
ISBN: 978-0756-635121 (Paperback)
ISBN: 978-0756-635138 (Hardcover)

Printed and bound in Mexico by R.R. Donnelley.

The publisher would like to thank the following for their kind
permission to reproduce their photographs:
(Key: a=above; b=below/bottom; c=center; l=left; r=right; t=top):
James Buckley Jr., 41; Ralph Clevenger: 38; Dreamstime.com (photographers listed):
Scorad 5; Bruce Macqueen 14; Yanik Chauvin 15t; Jhaviv 16; Scott Karcich 22; Holly
Kuchera 28, Stuart Duncan Smith 32t, Jeffrey Frey 36, Paul Cowan 37, Wessel DuPloy 40;
Getty Images, 17; iStock: 4, 18, 33, 36t, 42, 44; Photos.com: 8, 15b, 26, 30, 31, 32b, 39.
All other images © Dorling Kindersley Limited
For more information see: www.dkimages.com

Discover more at
www.dk.com

Contents

Searching for clues

You're on a hike in a beautiful forest. You stop to take a break and drink some water. The sun is shining, the trail ahead is clear, and you and your pals are having a great time. But you haven't seen any animals yet. A few bugs, sure, and some birds, but no cool critters you can brag about when you get home.

However, while you might not spot some of those animals, you can discover if they've been around. But it's not easy.

You have to look for clues, you have to seek the evidence . . . you have to think like an animal.

You have to become—a Nature Detective.

The animals of the world—forest, pond, seashore, wherever you are— are out there. Learning how to read their signs is a great way to enjoy the outdoors even more.

Just as you leave footprints when you walk, animals leave tracks, trails, and other things behind, too. Some of those things are left behind by accident.

A rabbit can't help leaving paw prints in soft dirt. A snake sliding through some soft mud leaves a trail. You can see where some birds have been by finding their feathers. Finding tooth marks in an acorn means a squirrel has been feeding there.

Other signs are left behind by animals on purpose. Some animals mark their territory by spraying scent (or even poop!). Wild cats or bears might make scratch marks on trees or logs to let other animals know that this is their place. Birds leave behind nests when they're finished with them.

Whether the
signs are left
behind by accident
or on purpose, you
can "read" them
if you know what
you're looking for.

Bird nest

Let's find out some of the ways
you can search for clues as a Nature
Detective . . . and find out what animals
have been all around you!

Rabbit tracks in the snow

Tracking down tracks

Walk down a trail and then stop for a moment and look behind you. What do you see that marks your progress? You'll probably see footprints. The tracks or prints left by animals' feet are often the easiest clues for Nature Detectives to find.

Animals leave tracks as they move through their habitat. These tracks can tell you where an animal has been and where it is going. You might also discover evidence of a chase.

Squishy site

A great place to look for tracks is near the edge of any body of water. The soft banks of ponds, streams, and rivers help tracks show up easily.

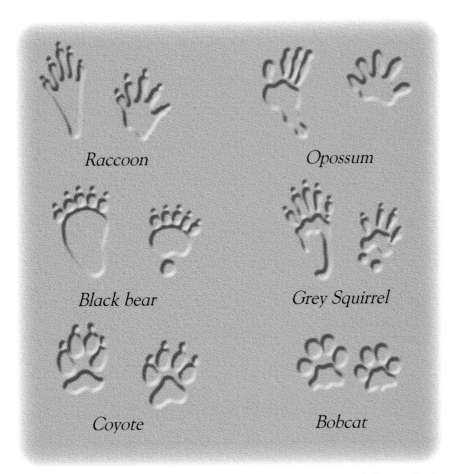

Animal tracks (not to scale) showing back and front feet.

For example, look for a predator's tracks going in the same direction as its prey. Bobcats, for instance, don't have their claws out when walking. When you see their claw marks that means you've spotted a sign of an attack!

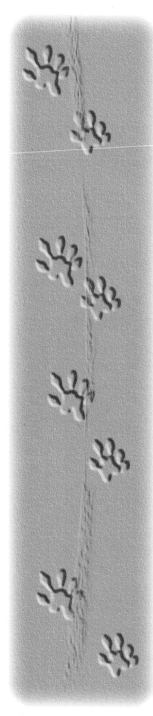

Otter tracks

You can learn a lot about an animal just from its footprints. A large print means a large animal, for instance, while smaller animals leave smaller tracks.

Bird tracks are very different than those made by animals with pads on their feet. Plus, you know a bird that swims is nearby if you see webbed feet. A bird track with thin "toes" is probably not a swimmer!

You might also see tracks other than those made by feet. A snake

An otter's tail leaves a mark between its footprints

will leave a long, thin trail as it glides
through dirt or mud. A frog might leave
a mark where it sat—that's right, a
butt-print. Some animals, such as otters,
drag their tails, so that the tracks have
a long, thin line between the paw prints.

The first thing you'll discover with any set of tracks is what direction they are pointing. Knowing which way an animal is going helps you follow its trail properly. Most animals have toes on the front of their feet. However, raccoons, for instance, have larger feet in front and smaller ones in back. And with

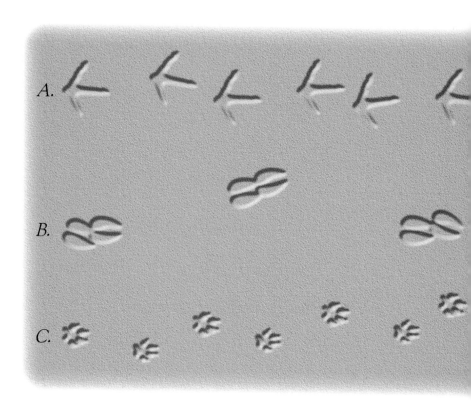

hoofed animals such as deer, you have to know which way is forward (hint: It's usually the pointy end of the hoofprint).

The tracks shown on this page are all moving from left to right across the page, for instance. Can you tell which animals made these tracks? The answers are on the next page.

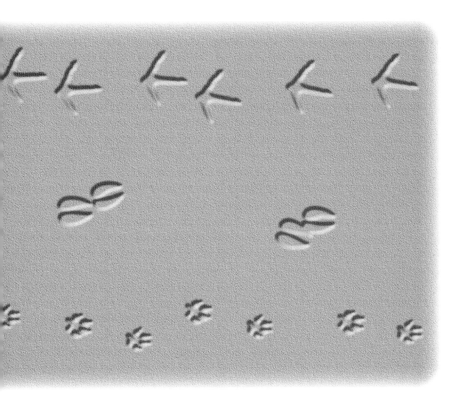

How many of these animals did you guess?

Another clue to look for when following tracks: How are the tracks arranged? Deer hoof prints that are close together means a walking deer.

If the prints are farther apart, that usually means it was running.

The prints of a dog and a fox are very similar. You can tell

A. Wild turkey

them apart, however, by how they are arranged. Fox tracks are in an almost straight line, while a dog's are next to each other.

B. White-tailed deer

You're not the only Nature Detective in the wild. Predators follow tracks and smells to find prey. Keep your eyes peeled for signs of where an animal has walked— or run away!

C. Red fox

Things they left behind

An important rule every hiker should follow is "Take only pictures and leave only footprints." Animals, however, don't have to follow that rule. They leave all sorts of things behind for Nature Detectives to discover.

For instance, you've probably seen your housecat make scratch marks on a

The sharp claws of a bear made these huge marks.

scratching post. Wild cats do the same thing, only their posts are real trees. Look for long scratches on tree trunks or large branches. These are to sharpen their claws, but also to let other cats know they're in the area.

However, scratches found high up on a tree (several feet above your head) probably mean a bear has done some scratching there.

Mountain lions, like housecats, love to scratch.

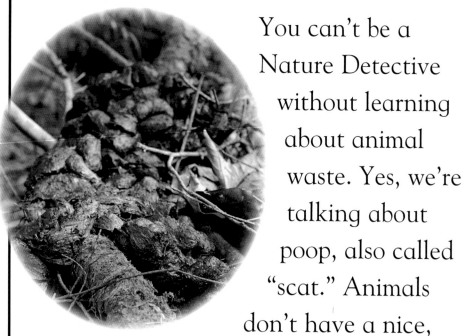

Bear scat

You can't be a Nature Detective without learning about animal waste. Yes, we're talking about poop, also called "scat." Animals don't have a nice, clean bathroom like you do at home. They poop where they live—in the forest or by the pond or from the air (like a bird).

Different animals leave behind different shapes; learning what those shapes are will help you identify the animals and what they eat.

Round droppings come from animals that eat plants. Longer droppings come

out of animals that eat meat (that is, they eat other animals). Bigger animals, not surprisingly, leave bigger poop.

Animals also leave their poop (and pee, or urine) behind to mark their territory, to tell other animals, hey, this is my place! (Rhinoceroses are very messy, flinging their poop all around with their tails!)

Rabbit droppings

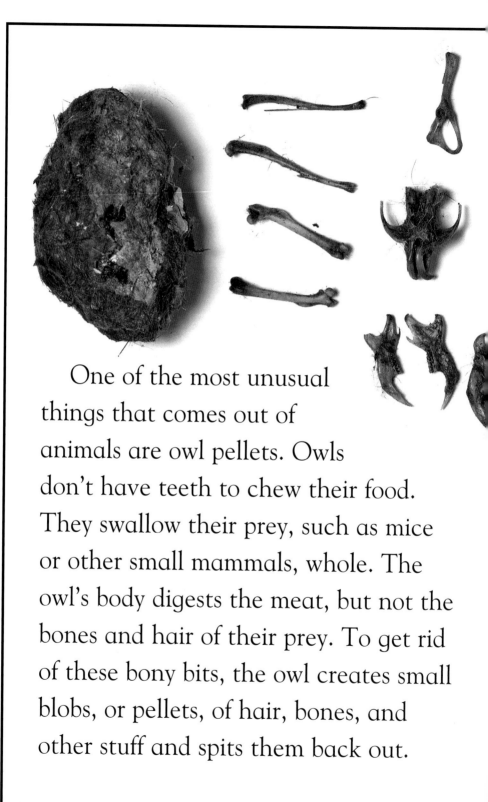

One of the most unusual things that comes out of animals are owl pellets. Owls don't have teeth to chew their food. They swallow their prey, such as mice or other small mammals, whole. The owl's body digests the meat, but not the bones and hair of their prey. To get rid of these bony bits, the owl creates small blobs, or pellets, of hair, bones, and other stuff and spits them back out.

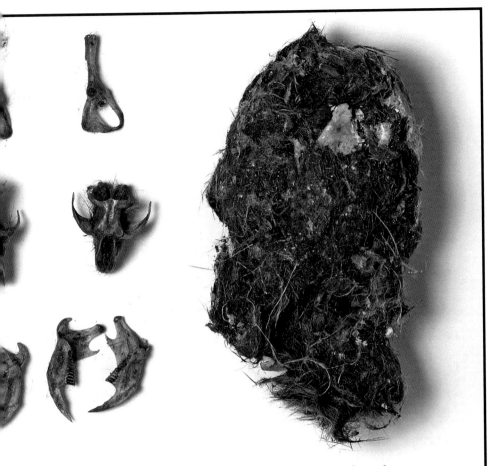

Two owl pellets and some of the bones found within.

It sounds kind of gross, but an owl pellet is like a little treasure chest for a Nature Detective. Look for a grayish, thumb-sized object. Break it open carefully to see the bones, skulls, and teeth of the animals that some lucky owl has recently enjoyed.

Tree with beaver damage

One animal leaves behind very unusual and obvious signs. Hard-working beavers chew trees, branches, and sticks while building their dams. Look for a tree stump chewed into a cone shape near a river or stream. A beaver probably did that to get construction materials. You might also see a beaver dam on a river or stream. Look for a pile of sticks and mud that blocks the flow of water.

Another type of animal leaves behind more than evidence of his work. Snakes leave their entire skins behind after they shed, which can be several times a year. They wriggle out of their old skins to reveal new skin and scales beneath.

Nature Detectives should look for very thin, snake-shaped casings on the ground. You can see the scales and ridges of the snake very clearly.

Snake skin after shedding

Who ate here?

While you always clean up after you eat, most animals don't! The signs of where an animal fed and what it ate are all around most habitats.

In the forest, look for acorns or nuts that have been chewed, probably by mice or small mammals. Pine cones with many of their leaves removed show that a mouse or squirrel has been around, chewing happily. A broken snail shell might be a sign that a bird enjoyed a gooey snack. Mushrooms in a tree? They're probably not growing there. A single mushroom in a tree might be thanks to a squirrel who didn't finish his lunch. On the somewhat "gross" side, you might find what's left of a bird after a predator has finished.

Grey squirrel

Raccoons often find food near the edge of streams.

Near a stream or pond, look for shells left behind by a hungry raccoon. They catch and eat crayfish. Using their nimble fingers, raccoons clean the shell off the little animals before enjoying the meat. They leave the empty shells behind for you to find.

At a seashore, look for mussel and clam shells that have been emptied by birds. You might find half of a fish; the other half is probably inside . . . another fish! Crab shells might also be leftover from something's dinner. (Crabs also molt like snakes, so your particular crab might still be crawling happily around!)

Evidence of seafood: Mussels, crab claws, and snail shells..

Did you smell that?

You find footprints with your eyes and listen for bird song with your ears. But what about your nose? Do Nature Detectives sometimes sniff out clues?

They sure do. The most obvious is (all together now)—the skunk! Skunks send out a powerful-smelling spray from glands near their rear end. That smell can stay around for a long time. If a skunk has sprayed nearby, you'll know it! They use the spray mostly for defense against larger predators.

The scent of a skunk can linger in an area for many hours. That's a clue that even a "nosy" non-detective can find!

Some other forest animals will also use scent in defense. Wolverines, mink, and weasels all have scent glands that can spray foul-smelling stuff on an attacker.

Certainly, however, the skunk is still the smelliest of the bunch. But some animals use their scents in other ways. Cats and deer, among others, spray their scent. You might not smell it, but other animals sure can.

Predators often use scent to track down their prey. Foxes, coyotes, wolves, and other similar animals can follow the scent of their prey for miles.

Deer (left) sniff for danger, while wolves nose out prey.

In the forest

While mammals are fun to look for in a forest, you'll probably see more evidence of birds. First, of course, you'll hear them. Bird songs are a great way to locate such animals. Look carefully—without that sound, you might not be able to find them camouflaged in the trees.

Hawk feather

If you can't hear them, look for other signs. Feathers dropped to the ground can tell you what sort of birds live in the area. A nest no longer being used is always a fun find. You might also find broken egg shells that a

Bird nest: Don't touch!

Woodpeckers have been here: Can you count the holes?

baby bird has left behind. (Make sure
never to disturb a nest with eggs in it.)

Woodpeckers are certainly loud, too!
If you can't spot them, you'll probably be
able to spot the holes they leave behind.
They peck the holes to search for bugs
and to make cozy homes for their young.

In some forests, another cool thing Nature Detectives can look for is buck rub. Male elk or deer, called "bucks," get new antlers each year. Those new antlers are covered with soft, fuzzy stuff called "velvet."

The bucks want to rub that stuff off in the spring. They do this by rubbing the branches on the rough bark of trees. You'll see small, bare patches on the trees where they rubbed the antlers. The patches are probably about as high as your chest or head. You might also see small clumps of the fuzzy velvet on the ground below these bare patches.

In the spring, look for antlers on the ground, too. When the animals get their new antlers, they leave the old ones behind . . . for you to find!

You can see the soft velvet still on this elk's antlers.

At the seashore

Seagull tracks

The shore of an ocean or larger lake has many special things for Nature Detectives to find.

The shells of many crustaceans, such as clams, mussels, and oysters, are often found on shore. Such shells might mark the spot of a bird buffet!

Can you tell when the tide is coming in and when it's going out? Look for wet sand far ahead of oncoming waves that signals an outgoing tide. If the waves are hitting dry sand, the tide is coming in.

Shells mark sea snacks.

At some beaches, you might see the unusual tracks left by sea turtles. Their big flippers make large divots in the sand, while their heavy bodies create a drag trail leading to the waves.

Kelp crab

Tidepools are great places to be a Nature Detective. Look for these shallow places an hour or so before or after low tide. Animals in ocean tidepools often use camouflage to blend with background. But knowing where they like to hide might help you spot them.

For instance, kelp crabs are the same color as light green kelp. Find the kelp and you might find the crab. Decorator crabs cover themselves with sea plants to help them hide.

Two sea stars and an anemone.

Octopi like to hide among small crevices in dark rocks; you probably won't find them hiding on a sandy bottom, for instance.

To locate sea stars, look near the tide line on the underside of ledges.

Seabirds called terns take flight on a windy beach.

Nature Detectives can learn about the weather by studying animals signs at the beach. Birds at the seashore take off by flying into the wind; that is, the direction the wind is blowing from.

So to see how the wind might have changed, look at the direction the tracks on the beach go. When the tracks suddenly stop, that might be where a bird took to the sky.

The sand on a beach can tell you about how old it is. The smoother the sand is, the longer that area has been a beach. Sand with lots of driftwood is often the site of heavy wave action.

Did you know there are dozens of types of seaweed? Messy piles of seaweed and other stuff is called "beach wrack." Looking through beach wrack, you can find shells, fish, crabs, bones, and, of course, all those types of seaweed.

This picture shows six types of seaweed on one beach!

Human signs

There are other animals out in the wild. You've seen them all around you. They walk on two feet and often leave behind far too many signs of their presence. Do you know which animals we mean?

That's right: People.

The signs of people are, sadly, found far too often in many wilderness areas. Wild animals are allowed to leave their "trash" behind, but people should never do that. Good Nature Detectives always look out for signs of these two-footed animals and pack out any trash they find. We've said it before, but we can't say it enough: When you're out in nature, take only pictures and memories—leave only footprints.

These are not the clues Nature Detectives like to see.

Leaving trash behind is a bad way people interact with nature. Another is when people disturb animals' homes. Being a Nature Detective and observing animals and the signs they leave behind is great. But it's never right to disturb or bother a wild animal. Take pictures with your camera, draw the scene with a pencil in your notebook, or just keep those memories in your mind.

The wild world is a wonderful place to explore.

Knowing what to look for will help
you learn more about it and enjoy it
more. Now, go become a great Nature
Detective and see what you can find!

Find out more

Here are some other books you can enjoy to learn more about looking for signs of animals while you become a Nature Detective.

Discovering Nature's Alphabet
By Krystina Castella and Brian Boyl
(Heyday Books, 2006)
The authors have turned a hiking game into a cool book. Using photographs of things found in nature, they take readers through the alphabet. Along the way, look for more signs of nature you can look for on your own hikes.

Follow the Trail: A Young Person's Guide to the Great Outdoors
By Jessica Loy
(Henry Holt, 2003)
From dried soup to nuts in trail mix, this all-in-one guide gives you the low-down to everything from tracking animals to packing for a camping trip.

Peterson First Guides: Birds, Butterflies, Wildflowers, Reptiles/Amphibians, etc.
By Roger Tory Peterson
(Hougton Mifflin, various years)
One of America's leading nature experts created these beginning guidebooks for animal spotters. They're perfect to take in your backpack for easy reference on the trail.

Here are some Web sites that you can visit to learn even more:

Boys' Life Magazine
www.boyslife.org
The magazine's "Outdoors and Gear" section includes all sorts of tips for Nature Detectives. Meet the Gear Guy, send in your nature photos, and find new articles on animals, nature, and the outdoors.

Nature Detectives in Great Britain
www.naturedetectives.org.uk
While some of the species of animals and plants will be different, this site from Great Britain has a lot of general outdoors tips and games for you to check out.

Tips from an Exert
www.bear-tracker.com
A real-life professional animal tracker put together this site, which includes tips on how to identify various animal tracks you might find.

Glossary

Buck
The male of species such as deer and elk.

Buffet
A form of dining in which the food is spread out on trays and plates for diners to choose from.

Camouflage
Skin, fur, or feather coloring or patterns that help an animal blend in with its surroundings.

Crevices
Tight or narrow spaces or cracks in rocks.

Crustacean
A type of marine animals with a hard outer shell and a pair of pincer or claws.

Detective
A person who uses evidence to discover something or to solve a crime.

Digest
Take food into one's body and change it into energy the body can use.

Dung
Solid animal waste.

Evidence
Information used to discover or solve something.

Glands
Body parts that send fluids into other parts of the body or out of the body.

Habitat
The area where an animal normally lives.

Molt
When an animal sheds its skin to replace it with new skin.

Predator
An animal that catches and eats other animals.

Prey
Animals that are eaten by other animals.

Scat
Solid animal waste.

Scent
A smell that can be detected by another animal.

Territory
A specific area of land.

Tide line
The point on the beach to which the sea advances at high tide.

Velvet
The name for the fuzzy stuff that grows on new antlers.